ON THE COAST

AND OTHER POEMS

ACKNOWLEDGEMENTS

Some of these poems first appeared in *Bim*, *Caribbean Quarterly*, *Savacou*, *Jamaica Journal*, *Breaklight*, *Impact* and *The Literary Half-Yearly*.

A NOTE ON THE TEXT

This republication of Wayne Brown's poems collects together all the poems that originally appeared in *On the Coast* in 1972, the poems published in *Voyages* in 1989 and one previously uncollected poem. Part I includes the poems from *On the Coast*, printed in their original order, but in the versions as printed in *Voyages* where Wayne Brown made small improvements in punctuation and layout and more occasionally in wording. He excluded three poems from *On the Coast* in *Voyages* ("Fir Tree", "A Sterner Approach" and "Sing Willow"). Two poems included in *Voyages* Part I ("Whales" and "The Visit") are printed at the beginning of Part II. Thereafter, the sequence (from "The Dark Jurors" onwards) is as printed in *Voyages*.

We called this collection *On the Coast and Other Poems* to pay respects to the now classic status of the volume that first announced Wayne Brown as a major poet.

WAYNE BROWN

ON THE COAST

AND OTHER POEMS

INTRODUCTION BY MERVYN MORRIS

P E E P A L   T R E E

On the Coast
first published by Andre Deutsch in 1972
Voyages
first published by Inprint Caribbean, 1989
This edition
first published by Peepal Tree Press Ltd 2010
17 King's Avenue
Leeds LS6 1QS
UK

ISBN 13: 9781845231507

Supported by
ARTS COUNCIL
ENGLAND

CONTENTS

II

INTRODUCTION

MERVYN MORRIS

I

I first met Wayne Brown late in 1966 when I returned to the University of the West Indies to be Warden of Taylor Hall. He was one of the outstanding personalities on the Mona campus, his brilliance widely recognized and sometimes resented. I was struck by his intellectual confidence and amused by a verbal playfulness I still consider characteristically Trinidadian. He was already committed to the special importance of the imagination, and wittily dismissive of anyone, including some of his teachers, who seemed to have other priorities. His early poems are often, at least in part, about creativity. "Something's underground alive" ("The Approach, p.21, this edition). The persona in "Remu" (a tide race) declares:

> I would write poems like mainsails drawn
> up the bent masts of motor schooners
> floundering in the remu's flow:
> held clear of that chaos, but quivering,
> holding the strain below. (p. 37)

He knew that the poet is not always in conscious control: the creative process (as in "The Thought-Fox"; Wayne often recommended Ted Hughes) requires watchful waiting. In a nicely ambiguous line (in "Soul On Ice") the persona is "the landscape shimmering, waiting for words" (p.59). In "Light and Shade" the poem

> ...is a wall.
> Or maybe a string

> Of mountains, out of whose blue haze
> may yet come (if I am patiently dumb)

> Hannibal, swaying slowly as his elephant sways." (p. 43)

7

In "The Witness" the "black nut in the surf" represents the poet, "that stranger by the sea" who is

> …your memory,
> that each sunset moves among
> the jetsam of the tribe, the years,
> widowed past grief, yet lingering… (p.67)

When Dennis Scott, Tony McNeill, Wayne and I, in unplanned meetings in the Warden's house, discussed each others' draft poems, Wayne would be more emphatic than the rest of us. He could be very challenging, not just about details in a poem but sometimes its aesthetic assumptions. Even when I didn't agree with what he was saying, the force of his attention was an energizing compliment. I didn't know it at the time, but he may have been remembering what he saw and liked in Derek Walcott's approach: "a certain high seriousness that doesn't have time for tact and caring about the person's feelings, but deals with what's on the page; that's unstintingly generous if you think they deserve it, and unstintingly critical if you think they don't."[1]

People who have been in workshops led by Wayne have spoken warmly of their usefulness. He led with authority. He was firm about requiring, *inter alia,* that members of the poetry workshop master the basics of metre – as a preliminary, if they chose, to writing good free verse – and that each week they learn by heart a great poem he had assigned. There was resistance from time to time. He recalled a "passionate and very loud" disagreement with a newcomer who questioned the value of learning poems by heart. "Next week," he told the man, "you will recite this poem or you will leave my house with your money."[2] Wayne could be combative, and unforgiving. Gratuitously disparaged by one of the founders of the Calabash Literary Festival, he parsed the public apology and, though he would publicize the annual event in the *Observer*, never once attended, though urged by friends to do so. He treated the suggestion with patrician disdain.

Until I read Kenneth Ramchand's piece in *Fifty Caribbean Writers* (1986)[3] I knew very little of Wayne's life before Mona. He was born in Port of Spain on July 18, 1944. His father, Kenneth Vincent Brown, was the first black Chief Justice of Trinidad and Tobago, and son of the first black Attorney General. His mother died giving birth to him. He lived with an uncle and an aunt until he was sent to boarding school at nine years old; from then until he was sixteen "home was the boarding school during term, with visits from the family on weekends"; at sixteen he went to live with his father "who treated him like an adult and sometimes like a boarder."[4] Which makes me recall some lines by Wayne I memorized while he was still at Mona: "My father lives in a house of stone. / His house is almost empty."

As a child, Wayne often spent time at an uncle's holiday home "on the wild and windy coast".[5] His deep connection with the sea and sea creatures is evident in many of his poems. As in "Mackerel":

> ...somewhere, hanging in streams
> of light, some ice-blue Purpose
> keeps in quiet its
> unfathomable self,
> given over, all
> over, with easy fins,
> to the timeless surge of the sea." (p.30)

In sixth form at St Mary's College he was influenced by his English teacher, Fr. Quesnel, who made his pupils write poems "in different stanzaic forms and modes and using specified metrical patterns."[6] It was he, Ramchand tells us, who first mentioned Derek Walcott to Wayne; and he gave him a copy of T.S. Eliot's *Selected Poems*. After leaving school, Wayne went to work as a sports journalist at *The Trinidad Guardian*, where Derek Walcott was covering the arts. Walcott talked with him, lent him books, and encouraged him to read Robert Lowell and Ted Hughes. A friendship developed. "It became normal," Wayne said, "for me to take a poem hot off the typewriter down to Derek and hear what he had to say about it."[7]

Wayne came to the Mona campus in 1965. He married Megan Hopkyn-Rees in 1968 and they divorced in 1981:

> ...the sentence stands. We never found
> words in which we could both live." ("Words", p.98)

Voyages, his second collection of poems (published in 1989), is dedicated to their daughters, Mariel and Saffrey.

His first collection of poems, *On the Coast* – dedicated to Derek Walcott – was published in 1972 by André Deutsch, who also published in 1976 *Edna Manley: The Private Years*, his biography of the sculptor whom he had come to know while studying at Mona. In 1975-76 he was the Gregory Fellow in Poetry at the University of Leeds. When he returned to the Caribbean the jobs he did included teaching literature at the University of the West Indies, in Trinidad and later in Jamaica. He edited *Derek Walcott: Selected Poems* (1981). For over sixteen years he conducted creative writing workshops in various places, including Port of Spain and Kingston. He taught, finally, in the MFA programme at the University of Lesley.

He was also a columnist. *In Our Time*, begun at the *Trinidad Express* in 1984, "was published in the Trinidadian, Jamaican and Guyanese press over its lifespan – upwards of 3,500 editions," in Lisa Allen-Agostini's obituary account. "He also wrote a short-lived column called *In the Obama Era* for six months in 2009. It followed the weekly series *The Race for the White House*, which appeared between February and November 2008 in the *Express*, the Barbados *Nation* and Guyana's *Stabroek News*."[8] He wrote elegant columns of unusual range – hard-hitting pieces on Trinidadian politics; informed analyses of United States foreign policy and the presidential race; polemics on American politics and the Iraq war; sensitive recordings of personal experience, and responses to literature and culture; praise-songs to genius (such as David Rudder, Brian Lara, Usain Bolt); mood pieces; short stories. "I write about anything," he said (in 1987) and "I use the techniques of fiction in writing these pieces."[9] Some of the columns are collected in *A Child of the Sea* (1989) and *Landscape with Heron* (2000), each subtitled "Stories and Remembrances". A new collection, *The Scent of the Past*, is to be published by Peepal Tree Press.

Diagnosed with lung cancer, Wayne confronted his prognosis with resignation and humour. To at least two of his friends he declared that he had looked at death and found it "doable". He went sailing as often as he could. He refused to give up smoking. To what he called his "valedictory workshop" in Jamaica he wrote, having journeyed to Boston to fulfill commitments to the MFA programme at Lesley University: "Y'all think I'm up here walking among the pine trees and thinking about the Hereafter, but I'm here bussing me ass with work."[10] "A month before he died," writes Lenworth Burke, "at the end of one class, Wayne announced that each of us could take five books from one of his bookcases. There was a rush and jostling and at least one of us, I'm sorry to say, took more than five. He chuckled his disapproval."[11]

He died on September 15, 2009. Most of the many tributes mentioned that he had been a poet, but the overwhelming emphasis was on his contribution as a columnist and a teacher of creative writing.

II

On the Coast, published in 1972, was a Poetry Book Society Recommendation and won the Commonwealth Poetry Prize the following year. *Voyages*, published in 1989, offered new poems and revised versions of most of the poems from *On the Coast*. The present collection – *On the Coast and other poems* – includes all the poems from the 1972 book, but in the revised versions approved by the poet.

The most consistent revision replaces upper-case with lower-case letters at the beginning of many lines, visually enhancing the flow. Punctuation is reconsidered. Occasionally, however, there are bigger changes. In "Noah", for example, a stanza read in 1972:

> Finally one bird, unasked, detached itself
> And battered around inside his skull.
> Thankfully Noah released it, fearful,
> Hoping, watching it flit and bang
> Against wind, returning each time
> Barren. Till one day, laden with lies,
> It brought back promise of fruit, of
> Resolution and change. (*On the Coast*, p. 32)

"Thankfully" is deleted: it was weakly ambiguous – Noah behaving thankfully, and the narrating persona seeming casually to say *thank-*

fully – and for no clear reason echoing "Finally" and anticipating "fearful". In the 1989 text "hoping" acquires greater rhythmic weight, and the isolation of "returning each time" gives sharper focus to the optimistic watching, disappointed (in both versions) in the emphatic first beat of the following line. The stanza now reads:

> Finally, one bird, unasked, detached itself
> and battered around inside his skull.
> Noah released it, fearful, hoping,
> watching it flit and bang against wind,
> returning each time
> barren. Till one day, laden with lies,
> it brought back promise of fruit, of
> resolution and change. (p. 47)

In terms of craft, Wayne got better as a poet. Between *On the Coast* and *Voyages* there is a continuity of concerns – love, time, history, race and class, self-discovery, sea, creative life – and the later poems are more assured. The work is, as before, replete with literary echoes – "Paradigm", for example, (pp.92-93) is a virtual tribute to 17th century English poets such as Lovelace and Marvell.

At least one of Brown's personae has "travelled far and witnessed many marvellous things" ("Voyages", p. 77). But where, in the end, is home?

> And I am an orphaned islander,
> on a sandspit of memory,
> in a winter
> of bays. I have no home." ("On the Coast", p.58)

In "Facing the Sea":

> I look at the water and cannot think
> *Home is where we start from – or*
> *Reaching no absolute in which to rest,*
> *one is always nearer by not keeping still,*
>
> until the woman starts up and points…" (p.79)

The voice in "Rampanalgas" muses:

> We are born here
> once only…
> …
> Now, years later, I watch this shack,
> the heart's first effort, rusting shut,
> and turn from the glass… (p. 81)

"The Dark Jurors", which opened section two of *Voyages*, is opposed to history as stasis.

> My dark jurors want to know
> where I am from: but I am dumb,
> finding no syntax to cement
> these stones and distant stars,
> nor noun but might mash up their monument
> of suffering as history.
> My jurors are patient. They offer me
> a wide range of tongues, like duelling
> pistols served on a rattling tray. (p. 76)

The "dark jurors" are peers of the persona checking his native credentials, "dark" suggesting that they (like him) are black and also hinting that they do not understand. Their challenge makes him think in terms of language – "syntax", "noun", "tongues" – and the search is ongoing ("I am dumb,/finding no syntax…/nor noun"). The search is for a language to bring together ground-level reality ("these stones") and "distant stars", symbolic of imaginative longing; "stones" also suggesting a burden which may make the imaginative enterprise more difficult. The Creole inflexion in "mash up" – in contrast to the formal English tone of "cement / these stones and distant stars" – seems to mock the presumed language preference of those who favour "suffering as history", with their solid, earthbound "monument" to stasis. When the poem goes on to say "My jurors are patient" we have to wonder whether the sense requires an emphasis on "My", to suggest a distinction between "My dark jurors" and these other jurors, the ones who offer him "a wide range of tongues". But perhaps they overlap, and the poem ends in a simile of deadly contest: "a wide range of tongues, like duelling / pistols served on a rattling tray."

"Quinam Bay", somewhat similar in attitude but more polemical, drew heavy fire. The poem, in memory of Eric Roach and "after reading the eulogies", begins

> Roach gone, the carrion
> that drove him, hurt hawk, from the echoing air
> with their hunger for bloodbath, their shrill caws
> of treachery,
> shriek with excitement.
> Dead, and to them he is Hero.
> Carrion like them dead.   (p.90)

Gordon Rohlehr, in an extensive counter-attack, deems Wayne's apprenticeship to Walcott "parasitic."[12] Wayne's early poems do indeed make gestures of acknowledgement to "a very great poet"[13] – there are echoes and allusions – but there is more to them than that.

Wayne was wrongly perceived by some as one of those people always promoting European literary standards to the disadvantage of Caribbean vernacular experiment. His actual position was: "There's very good dialect writing and there's junk. Most of it is junk – just as most of Standard English writing is junk. But the milieu in which this thing is being discussed is so simplistic and crass, really, that I look long and hard to find a critic who'll say, 'Look at how gloriously Dennis Scott uses dialect in "Uncle Time" and how spendthrift and wastefully and uninspired this other one uses dialect in . . . "Jah Dub" ', or whatever the hell it is."[14] He used to tease me by pretending he could not accurately pronounce the name Mutabaruka. But he could also be impatient with self-deprecating English attitudes. "England, Autumn" wonders whether

> . . . Truth, highflying, doesn't still
>
> on occasion stoop from a smoking sky,
> or an imperilled mortal "I"
> break from your carapaced "one".

The poem seems to be defending Walcott, who isn't actually mentioned:

> But, doesn't heaven
> prophesy still over England?
> Since when was lightning ironic,
> or thunder without sonority?
>
> You ought to walk with me, critic,
> . . .
> You should ask more of literature… (p.103)

Many an Englishman, he implies in "Critic",

> Takes rain, the racket
> in a madman's head
>   and strains
> it into sonata. (p.105)

He writes poems about being an outsider in cold London ("her silhouette / knows, the Ripper was black, was black ("Snow", p.61). In "Trafalgar Square"

> …Moss grows
> from her navel and breasts.
> If I shared her history, Greek like the rest,
> I'd share that foetid anchorage too.
> Must keep moving… (p.50)

Poems such as "Soul On Ice", "Snow" and "Trafalgar Square" raise issues of race and class in England. "Red Hills" is set in Jamaica:

>   …Red hill scar, red
> nigger preserve,
> our roses bloom whitely here. (p.63)

In "Wide Sargasso Sea" there is manifest sympathy for white and near-white people where "the sea gleams, the Negroes erupt, / the woman waits by the improbable stile (p.65)." In its revised version the poem is offered "In memory of Winnifred and Gertrude Vincent-Brown".

The poems which refer to love say, mostly, *We were happy once.* Men must learn "to live at last / without such punctual heartbreak" ("The Bind", p.109). It is hard "to call the ocean / 'ocean' without her" ("In Real Life", p.90). Or to receive "A Letter from Elizabeth" stirring a memory of many years ago: "I could have lived forever in her gaze / as in a sunstruck, languorous season" (p.88). In "On the Coast":

> You came to me here, bewildered girl,
> your body warm and heavy with sleep.
> . . .
> Island girl, I am scared, don't leave me. (p.57-58)

But some of the partners – the "unextraordinary small-town girl", "one student nurse" ("Facing the Sea", p. 79) – seem less important than that. Wayne is reported to have told a workshop: "If you have a choice between swimming in the sea and not swimming in the sea, swim. If you have a choice between having sex and not having sex, have sex."[15] There is a voice in "Paradigm" saying: "Others have called this continence / sweet sorrow – I cannot –" (p.93). The poems know some of the pitfalls of commitment.

> She says *My life is yours* and means *I fear,*
> He says *I shall protect you* and means *own…"*
> ("The Lovers", p.97)

But love in "Prose" endures in difficult circumstances: we glimpse an elderly couple embracing at the docks:

> … his feet faltered all the way
> down the long gangplank; and her hair
> when wind or his unsteady hand unscarved it,
> was already grey. (p. 110)

Death figures less in this collection than in many. But there are elegies in celebration of creative people: Eric Roach ("Quinam Bay"), Nabokov, Pablo Casals and Picasso ("Dead in one month, the two Pauls", "Autumn Elegy", p.111). The final poem, "The Briefing", says goodbye for all of us:

May your flight be faultless and your hand
obey you at the last.
May you find your lost companions. (p. 113)

Endnotes

1. Verna E. George, "Conversation with Wayne Brown", *The Caribbean Writer*, Volume 21 (2007), p. 203.
2. George, p. 205.
3. Kenneth Ramchand, "Wayne Vincent Brown", in Daryl Cumber Dance (ed.), *Fifty Caribbean Writers: A Bio-Bibliographical Critical Sourcebook* (New York: Greenwood Press, 1986), pp. 83-95.
4. Ramchand, p. 85.
5. Ibid.
6. Ramchand, p. 87.
7. George, p. 203.
8. Lisa Allen-Agostini, "Comprehensive Wayne Brown Obit" (internet, temporary).
9. Wayne Brown interviewed by Peter Nazareth, University of Iowa, October 27, 1987.
10. Lenworth Burke, "An Honoured Guest", *Jamaica Journal* Vol. 32, No. 3 (February 2010), p. 61.
11. Pp. 61-62.
12. Gordon Rohlehr, *My Strangled City and Other Essays* (Port-of-Spain: Longman Trinidad, 1992), p. 150.
13. George, p. 203.
14. George, p. 223.
15. Burke, p. 61.

I

'He had come from a town on the coast they knew to found and settle, be baptized again, as well as to baptize, a new colony.'

Wilson Harris: *Palace of the Peacock*

THE APPROACH

A deepening evening, a quiet town,
A landscape flickering like candlelight –

Who moved the mountain?

The mountain squats suddenly at your ear, so close
You could almost touch it!
In its lee-dark there is a pit
That was not there before, that moves

Like whales grazing sargasso,
Like a memory advancing in swathes,
A pit that goes on widening
Itself, and taking slow hold of

The lime trees, the river, the asphalted road,
All that you say you own.

Something's underground alive.

And that's all you need to know
For now: how you come down
Is your business.

You may turn on all lights, you may turn to TV,
You may pray in your pillow, "Shall it be war?"
You may ask of the woman, "How shall I plead?"
You may cry, "Lift me, mother!"

You may cry, "Bury me, stars!"

I am the horse that has killed its owner.

I am the flesh in the dark.

THE TOURISTS

"The sun works for the Tourist Board"
was a bad joke. But now each noon
the sun toils like a fisherman
with a hard tide to beat
or a farmer whose wife will drop soon.

And in truth the beach is replete
with strangers. Each one arranges
tenderly his limbs for those brass rays
as a woman, testing each pose, changes
into nothing for her lover's gaze.

The natives mind their own business.
Some blond types are at it again.
An English anthropologist
praises the texture of a seine.
The sea's heard it all before.

A scene from a tourist brochure.
Under that sun
all is languor, and those who come
will find nothing unusual, not
one gesture or motion overdone

But for one parrot fish which turns
grave somersaults on the stainless steel
spear that's just usurped its dim
purpose; which was to swim
as usual through blue air, in silence, like the sun.

CONQUISTADOR

Entonces es que estoy verdaderamente,
verdaderamente lejos...?
(Pablo Neruda: "Las Furias Y Las Penas")

Old man
of the colonies
of hope, one beak
is seeking us.
I think
of your nightmare
cities: El-
dorado, and then
Madrid; then of those
poems like arrowing birds
migrating north along the wires
of a sun's eclipse
in that bad time...
Father, the wind's
grey-bearded these days,
and each washed-out moon
watches the bird's arrow like a bat
collapse, as our leaning horizon, the sea,
backed by no mountains such as yours,
collapses daily,
but always there is more...
Therefore, like poor
fishermen, when the tide goes
we scour the shoreline for its news:
black driftwood, a starfish, the eyeless corpse
of one whose hope, like ours, dipped
strangely; like moon, poem, bird;
and wait for the bottle
to bring the Word.
Brave poet, lost echoing
voice of the Andes,
not only our land
is levelled by this sea...

MONOS

Those yachts that dip as idly as kites,
trailing laughter like empty beer
bottles in their crinkling wakes

do not disturb this sea's breathing,
nor quicken its pulse
of dull, slippery fish, off Monos.

Over their kingdom, unaware, I camp
my silver shining skiff, a cloud.
Like a tainted anthropologist,

tattooed with Mary, my white queen
of heaven, I let down
rusted candelabra of roots

to probe the world below,
to find a foothold there.

I watch the sent cable, metal
beads, snarl on the gunwale
and stop.

The echoes do not rise.
Instead, my wracked bent senses
swarm with the formal organized
throb of the Yacht Club's missives.

The skiff's contrived navel string
trembles towards contact, and goes slack.
Graceful and helpless as a girl
the oiled hull falls, and rises.

It's all
a waste of regatta time. These creatures
have their own lives.

And even if I
should sink naked into their mists
how could I think

that this migrating Ishmael's
soul
that drowned, crushed, in some galley's hold

and next was lifted up on a white
peopled chain of sterilized buoys
(Monos, Huevos, Patos, the Rock)

could meet these quiet monsters on those grounds
of indifference such
as only common knowledge breeds?

"We left
somewhere a life we never found,
customs and gods"… So some poet preached.

And still – when I reach
my arm up to its banlon'd sleeve
into that numbed chaos,

all I think
is of another shore, moist
in sunshine, long

ago; then of one
beached, quiet fish
opening and closing useless jaws.

DEVILFISH

Fat butterfly, fleshed in sin,
fat Nazi.
Daily they climb

away from it, these wide-eyed fish,
break surface in octaves of scattershot, guns.
They'd choose a green nightmare any day by far

to its thick, whitening
absence. Ice-white, whiter
than thighs, than milk,

men in retreat utterly exhaust themselves.
In the end, caps in hand, falling
in, we enter its gaze, the gloom-cell.

Spent anxious Christians, we're taken in,
we endlessly extend
its dream.

Now, stuffed up like God, the state,
on us, the sea's
lumpen-proletariat,

it gathers its nightmare in and hurls it-
-self into our shattering air.
Marching in pairs no one sees

the wintering stream of it erupt,
nor hears the thunder of its
recoil:

and the fisherman, riding a storybook calm,
whistles for luck as he sends his lure down.

CRAB

Last evening in the living bay
ocean's arena sweated white,
greasing its gladiators. Waves,
excitable as spinsters,
gossiped along crack-scarred tiers
until the sun's torch dipped.

A lizard hurls its tongue out over the lake, gleaning
live flies; sharks rattle a teeming
fishpot; but the crab,

crouched on the jetty's last blind step, flayed
by drenching tide, grips
rock and stiffens,
drowning vaguely like the slow surge of dreams.

For him the oceanbed bares her breast, him
her tresses brush against,
who, squatting drunk beneath darkening surges,
        finally
breathes water.

Next morning, squadrons of gulls
swoop with the sun from eastern hills
and over the trenched sea.
The fishermen's putt-putt

ploughs like a solitary lawnmower through the gulf,
splashing sound across this hut
like a younger heartbeat, a song.

To the crackle of coffee
we push out the windows.

In the bay the last step dried in the sun,
breathing the stench of rancid hair,
tarnishing. There was no crab there.

MACKEREL

For Tony and Olive McNeill

Deeper, running
deeper, dropping
away, slipping
the clutch of our cold sun,
the driven shoal: all but one
who stayed, turning blandly
about the same calm plaque of sea
on a casual quest, forgetting time.

From the shelf of a rank, barnacled rock
I watched him: vague-tailed, in-
different, almost a drifting crease of blue,
he seemed for a time at ease: secure
with his secret, and indolent with knowledge,
and all given over to the surge of the sea.
                    Then
lost, in a quick panic, beating
left and right, an addict
scouring his place for some misplaced fix,
spun by the under-
waves of time.
                    Finally,
steadied as by a new
purpose, he sank, fin-thrilling.
His curled blue back shone
once in a crackle of sunlight and was gone,

and I, staring, peering from my shelf
with the curiosity of a child and a child's
horror, knew he would not return, though the wild
cheated gulls churned overhead, screaming.

The green crystal of our nether world
yielded nothing now. Yet
men will have their truths, their tidy legends,
their ends: so I

imagine him, risen elsewhere,
thrown ashore where the white wave spills
and cooling, his glass eye dulled,
or crammed to the gills
in the craw of a shark,
or thrashing, culled,
on the end of a line –

and only deny
that somewhere, hanging in streams
of light, some ice-blue Purpose
keeps in quiet its
unfathomable self,
given over, all
over, with easy fins,
to the timeless surge of the sea.

BALLAD OF THE ELECTRIC EEL

When Earth slept, like a pig in the sun
bellying out of its warm mud in places,
eel lay at the bottom of the ocean
like a shambles of coils in an empty carpark
or a magnet: one root for the sea's motion.

Dispossessed while sleeping by sunlight and wave,
woke to a waterworld poisoned with fish
some bigger than himself. When the whale's cave
loomed over him, eel had to bite the dust.
That was his first and last lesson. Learned fast,

fell into slices, sent his tail end
landward to reconnoitre while he watched from the weeds.
When the serpent went down under Woman's heel, eel
laughed toughly, like Widmark, and grew a reef.
Now he was bedded in rock.

Fish flourished, the coral reef
worked like a seacraft riding on oil.
Eel was its systems' analyst.
His eyes screwed down to far stars in space,
his jaws fell open like compasses, he set out

to run the world strictly by impulse.
Now he is king of the mineral dark,
Earth's ticking time bomb, inset like a diamond.
When he glides from his cave the tide climbs abruptly,
waves sever a headland, and men wage wars –

when he withdraws
long currents drag whole streets empty,
and men in mid-sentence stand and gape
like machines,
their brains gone completely blank.

INSOMNIA

The mule's shadow slackens. The moon is rusting
after so many bloodbaths in windy places,
so many encounters in air. You can hear
the ocean sloshing its sink, working in the dark without wages,
the cliffs like mad uncles standing fast at wars standing fast
over the nothing.

And in other stone-damp rooms
the woman and your child, asleep,
their fallen faces veiled and drained
by the mosquito netting,
have left the old house to its familiar sorrows, and to yours.

Ticking, ticking, the grandfather clock's trying
to turn itself to stone. The fridge's epileptic fit
shakes the house shortly, like a train.
There are moths like dead embers around the lamp's flame
and you've reached page four hundred and sixty.
Dear God, a whole life shrunk to this – !

You rise and pace –

And stand, slack-jawed, staring
like a just-dead man trying
to haul himself back along a memory
he cannot quite remember,
some tiny, drifting, sickle fact
from which his fate depends…

The muddy footprints on the stone floor
lead to *their* rooms and back out through the door,
        that's still ajar.

SONG FOR A SHIP'S FIGUREHEAD

Spirit of the forest, sufferer
now, Amazon might have shielded her
once in its most secret places: dank overgrown

groin
luminous belly
slate Arawak cheekbones –

her kingdom is earth
Earth

Now she scythes as the bowsprit scythes,
black broken branch to which she's been
lashed by these fire-haired sailors between

their long-limbed Miss Americas
and the ocean's milling.

On the rack of a rainbow
upturned she learns
a pitiless virginity,

Knees welded closed.

And the fishscales ascend,
ascend, she surrenders
her thighs to the sea's whispered kisses,

finally the belly: impenetrable, mailed.

She'll bear no one's bastards, that's for sure,
having lost her original kingdom.
Bent on extinction she rides secure.

For her breasts' black milk
has been salted and dried,
her nipples are only
weapons now, shearing, hurling the ocean

over her shoulder she strains she
hauls

at last her tormentors' quivering hulk
clean off the map's page
and into some inhuman age
sealed from each schism –

By day light flakes from her shoulders,
by night the phosphorus trails,
untethered from time she shall not die,
but over the crew's foolishly lolling

heads, her silhouette's risen claw
plunges and rears in the space between stars,
and finds the moon's face, and savages it

unceasingly: but neither will give in.

DROUGHT

The woman is barren. And the blackbirds
have had a hard time this year with the drought
and fallen like moths to the field's floor.

The woman is barren. And the city,
crawling south like an oil-slick,
will soon be around her ankles.

So she sings: "Will you marry me?
I will go searching under many flat stones
for water of the departed rains."

Sings, "O World, will you marry me?"

The riverbed's dried up completely, the lizards
have taken to the trees, to the high branches.
The cane rolls westwards   burning   burning

In the sunset of her time, in the ploughed crater
where the woman like a frail apostrophe
dances palely each evening

Among the fallen blackbirds.

REMU*

1

Cleopatra, washed up nude, sprawled
among the sphinxes. That last bite
and spring-tide of love she chose herself
floated her buttocks and rippled her thighs

Till the remu let her drop and slewed
north, eating Mediterranean.

2

When the oilslicks of the north
crawled south to die on island shores
         the remu
went underground. Rose under Peru.

3

If one day this dull-eyed sea
between the barracks and Gasparee
should boil as at a sharks' feast, know:
the remu is passing, mulatto.

4

By love deceived you backed off from
the remu's subterranean whim.
Now your only child is dying, look,
ague shaking him!

5

Maxie drown in de Dragon Mout'.
Fish beating, so he put out.
Greedy make he forget de sun.
Remu take he an' gone.

* A tide-race

6
America and Africa
hurled themselves apart,
twin cliffs in the nightsky's blue.
Between them rose the islands,

Between them raced the remu, like panzer men
through the Ardennes, already in France.

7
I see a child's hand
swept among waves
where the remu swings
to the open north.
Ah, Mittelholzer!

8
I would write poems like mainsails drawn
up the bent masts of motor schooners
floundering in the remu's flow:
held clear of that chaos, but quivering,
holding the strain below.

TRIP

1

The dog's exhausted. Its head
snarled in a kerosene tin,
it threads the dark skyline for miles
then stops. Flames break from its black
skull, as from a Moses rock,
in one towering column.
This is our burning cenotaph.

2

From far, sound of the sea.
Where the rain came down
mist seeps from the fields.
The earth is a furnace.
The women in white
are no virgins. The mist flows
through them till they're out of sight.
The trees take their places like stars.
The earth's plaque rides on its ooze.
How everything brims and trembles!

O God, what am I
to walk without scars
among all these, my
thoughts still on the moon?

VAMPIRE

1
Somewhere between midnight
and the moon's going
it wakes, clammy, from its bed of hairs

and thirsty. And turns
on its dream of blood
with a distended limp.

The white moon sentries its waking.

2
The moon's etchings
tilt and change
as the beast climbs awkwardly.

And the night was a cascade of lovers,
and the wind was the voice of the tribe, crying
'O give him back to the graceful dark!
O let him belong!'
                    while the moon sheds
like silks from Salome its torn clouds
and wind like a hand in the bowing trees
shakes all equally –

The night convulses, one cell heaves free,

and blinded by thirst the vampire goes,
a bloodclot in darkness, hurtling –

3
World without moon.

The bat's abroad.
The thick earth, drenched in darkness, sucks
at the valves of night like a wild child.
The dark drains visibly.

Now what strains through the thinned
air is the hallucination of its fear:
fields, a few trees, by morning mist dimmed —

How strange and bright and terrible is
the uninhabitable landscape that swims clear!

BOULDER

for Dennis Scott

Not from reverent fingers swung
into a claw an instant from
transubstantiation – nor

the monolithic mask of some
denuded sculptor wind and rain
were blurring back to beginnings:

That boulder.

How many seasons had it passed,
resisting metamorphosis?
I stared at it as into deep space.

Far off, pines waved in the lunar glow.
A river roared under cover.
The river has its hoarse voice still,

as, under wind, the mouths
of the dead thrust up into tree-boles.
So they might rage at the moon.

But this boulder shouldered off
tree, river and moon, each hurrying
thing – and one poet, come to try

his anthropomorphic graffiti,
felt the star in his reared wrist wink
out, his skull an ocean moon

drift off and leaves its fists of waves
unclenched, inert,
at the foot of some featureless coastline.

41

PASSING OUT

Suddenly the whole world crowds the equator.

Like sheep in rain
we close in, leaning laxly, while the light drains
westwards through pores, and is emptying
eyesockets of everything they contained

When this travelling darkness
moves up like infantry under cover
of lingering: clambering

Over the twilit rocks and watery horizon
like an exiled octopus with a sack trailing ink
or a solitary horseman

In Africa.

LIGHT AND SHADE

1
These potted plants
grow like your child
unfurling: all on the light's side.

2
Bookshelves: their lining
of memories, leaning
together or apart
like small plantations:

A bandstand in the forest
the musicians left
at sunset, leaving their music

and a brown girl trapped
in the moon's net.

3
I am ten years older
and each year still
besotted by sunlight.

4
This poem is a wall.
Or maybe a string

Of mountains, out of whose blue haze
may yet come (if I am patiently dumb)

Hannibal, swaying slowly as his elephant sways.

CAT

1
In the Beginning
the cat
watched for a while from the edge of the world.
On the seventh day
it moved in,
like your dead neighbour's, casually.

2
Adam and cowering Eve
felt the eyes watching and vainly tried
to cover their privates: but all that night
the cats streamed in through the garden gate.

3
Noah, while the others stood round in pairs,
reached forward to greet the bird with the branch.
But the cat killed it
with one slap.

4
The white cat's eyelids slide shut.
The Alps are completely snowed under.

5
Antony dead, the woman dead,
Rome hushed and waiting, emptily –
the cat stalked out of the palace.

6
O daughters of Africa,
your warriors are slain.
The night is a black cat
with yellow eyes.

7

Arthur, cantering back to the castle
after an exhausting peace,
noticed a cat trapped halfway
up a treetrunk.

8

Whether what woke you sounded like
a dropped nailfile,
or a bottle,
or the night of the sailors, think:
the cat's in your garbage,
woman.

9

Five hundred Viet Cong captured.
Race riots erupt in Atlanta.
Glancing sideways, hurriedly crossing the lit street,
the cat loped off
down an alley.

10

Dying in his sleep, one step past death,
heard the love-scream of cats and made
a terrible effort to sit up.

11

The morning after the bomb
was dropped, I woke early.
Silence past stillness, the city in ruins –
my hand touched fur and the cat purred.

NOAH

for Mervyn Morris

Everywhere fish wheeled and fled
or died in scores, floating like eggs.
From his mind's ark, Noah,
sailor for the kingdom of Truth's sake,
watched the water close like mouths
over the last known hills. Next day
he slept, dreaming of haystacks.

Water woke him. He stood, arms folded,
looking out of a porthole, thinking nothing,
numbed to a stare by horizon's drone, and the
dry patter of rain. On the third day,
decisive, sudden, he dragged
down the canvas curtain and turned
inward to tend his animals, his
animals, waking with novelty.

Locked, driven by fatigue, the ark
beat and beat across the same sea,
bloated, adrift, finding
nothing to fasten to.
Barnacles grew up the sides like sores. Inside,

Noah, claustrophobic, sat and watched
the occupants of his ark take on
new aspects, shudder into focus, one
by one. Something, he thought, must come
of this. Such isolation! Such concentration!
Out of these instinctual, half-lit lives,
something: some good, some Truth!
That night a dropped calf bawled to its feet,
shaking off light like dirt.

Noah, an old man, unhappy, shook
his head. Birth was not the answer,
nor death: his mind's ark stank
of birth and death, would always,
sundering, stink. Outside,
the hard insistent patter of rain
saying "Think, Noah, think! Break this
patter of rain, man!"
                          But only animals
moved in his mind.
                          Now, unbodied by raindrops,
the patter continued, empty, shelled,
clambering down along itself like crabs.
Driven, impotent, he neared despair.

Finally, one bird, unasked, detached itself
and battered around inside his skull.
Noah released it, fearful, hoping,
watching it flit and bang against wind,
returning each time
barren. Till one day, laden with lies,
it brought back promise of fruit, of
resolution and change.

Now animals and men crowded the gangplank,
peering eagerly about the returning hills
for some sign of change. Noah conducted them,
drifting among valleys with breaking smiles,
naming, explaining, directing: Noah, released,
turned once more outwards, giving thanks.

Relief dazed them: nobody realised
nothing had changed. Animal and man
settled quietly to old moulds, un-
remembered seasons of death and birth,
led by the bearded one, the prophet, Noah

rejuvenated, giving thanks on a hill,
moving among known animals and men
with a new aspect, giving thanks… While,
leaking, derelict, its mission abandoned,
the ark of his mind
wallowed empty westward
to where all rainbows
drown among waves

RILKE

for Edna Manley

For seven years, eyesockets like caves,
he watched in the mountains over the city
for the coming of the printless beast. But
in his mind's known home, continued usual,
order undisturbed: the cushioned cat,
the twitching dog asleep on the mat,
and his fed fire, private, stern,
keeping its anguished monologue of coals,
small poems in the lessening light.

Now past his prime, he watched at night
the logbook thicken with his soul's
entries, the low controlled fire turn
strange shapes off its silent walls.
He could discern nothing. The flagged hall
echoed, vacant, gaunt. Outside, wind leapt
howling in the trees; an evil mist crept
inward. He rose and dragged his wooden chair
as close to the fire as he dared.
From here there was nowhere to go.
Would the animal never rise?

The poems, he knew now, were lies,
bright, hot-pawed, skittery cats
cuffing, triumphant, out of old corners
dead roaches into the light. Yet on nights
when the moon like water rose to his eyes
and the fire sank into its pit, some ghost-
dog's howl, old as the hills, would sink
inward on ribbons of wind, and, shaken, he
would think : "Time for another log." Might not

A little fire, small poem, save him?
Somewhere, someone was lying still.
                                        So
for seven years he stayed, enfolded in mist
but mesmerized, dulled by that same fire's glare
that kept the animal out. But one night
exhausted, slept on his chest, coals
tiny as stars, and the animal entered.

All night in nightmare he dreamt of the wail
of the wind, taking new shapes within him
like flames; and next day was sure he'd glimpsed
(too briefly for charting, it left no trail)
the shadow of a great, unkempt beast
bounding through billowing veils of mist,
the poem swung like a kite at its tail,

Crying in the teeth of the wind.

FIR TREE

for R. D.

At night, distracted, over the town
something goes winging where the old fir tree
keeps its memory still.
It is only the wind, you coolly point,
over our initials, turning leaves.

The book leafs back
to white mornings and the smell of grass,
your swinging plaits, the grinning dog
that ran before us, puppy-bright,
and one other, vaulting in boyhood
over an ominous bar of light.
You clapped and raised it a notch. Ten feet.

Another valley. Another ridge.
Then: "I must be home. Why? Because. Because
it is late. Late."

Oh yes, it was late, the sun said so,
but only your mother cared then.
The clock was lying in wait.

"As this etched tree
endures with our names
we shall endure forever."
                              And the sun
in the high leaves, dimpling and passing,
the sun in the thicket, gone.

It is late now, passing late, beyond
the time of the sun. The moon crawls
in the roof of our cave.

In the dark
the fir tree is singing to itself.
Its carved heart breaks between us.

Not even your wicked grin can save us now.

A STERNER APPROACH

for Jennifer and Tom Yew

Hate heaving its metal hub,
the aircraft, roaring, robs me of
your last lipped farewell. No matter.
Where we stand on the waving gallery

The wild fanned air smells of the sea,
smells of hair on your bare
shoulders, sweat-wet, gleaming on sand.
Against the high wind a seagull waves.

Now an attendant holds the door,
grinning like any pimp. Then
the ant-queue out to the waiting
plane, it in a frenzy, howling.

The forced physical fact of parting
hews at a faith still only half
renewed. Chilled, I turn to see
you backing away from glass.

My multiplying thoughts flake off,
go rolling, blown like fishscales
over the tarmac.
You must learn to preserve yourself, and care…

Over the open space we hasten,
over the open space the wind
and the sun
putting its X on the pitch as I stop and wave

At the gangway. The mind uncovers
one last, lifting, half-peeled thought:

"Time for a sterner approach to love",
and I am on the threshold. Scared,

Withhold, then plunge
into the belly of the quivering thing.
Within, some dog, some trampled soul
shrieks and withdraws.

Slamming shut, the easy door
shatters the windshield of her smile.
The icy corridor wrings down
on silence. Not even a backwash of fear.

I do not care if we crash.
I do not care

SING WILLOW

For Megan

To this island, urged by the pushing
sea, you, strumpet, were early borne.
Your tall nursemaids
whispered obscenities like hummingbirds

At your quick ear and vanished, leaving you
stripping a butterfly, practising words.
Combers for dialogue grew in your side.

Frowning, bared, upon cyclical tides
you learnt from the start
the pure myth of choice:
you built your child's castles of smooth white stones.

One day the trickle of bad men began.
You giggled and ran
backward through bush to the waterfall, where,
crouched like a carving, each hand to a breast,
you suffered black towering dreams like cliffs

in the whitening moon, a big girl growing...

Each morning the sun between your thighs
unravelled the beach, that diary where
you numbered the hulks shipwrecked among your castles.
So you became your island.

That when, on a low rusting dawn,
one sea-blackened sailor, ram on the wind,
came tacking and cresting towards your delta,
to what minstrelsy of nursemaid, comber and fall

Did your tides draw him on, in clear light,
to what fabulous landfall, and
you, Desdemon,
the rivermouth silting after his wake, like history?

ON THE COAST

... words which love had hoped to use,
Erased with the surf's pages.
(Derek Walcott, "Islands")

1

The light founders. Rain puckers the ocean.
I see a small town, found, then forgotten,
rusting in silence by a sea's edge
where liners no longer come.

You came to me here, bewildered girl,
your body warm and heavy with sleep.
Your eyes were calamitous waters.
How grave were your admonitions!

Later you spoke to me quietly,
as at a distance or under rain
the sea nuzzles its sandspit.
You were beautiful, and I loved you.

Will you never be home again?

2

The warehouse on the waterfront
is empty tonight. The ocean shines.
Moon, it is a winter moon,
a moth's wing netted in cloud.

Why do I sit up these late nights
barefooted on a broken pier?
I never saw galleons enter the moon,
nor the great house that burned on the hill,

57

and the unpunctual fisherman
who came out of nowhere suddenly
rounding the point on long oars,
had nothing to say to me.

Night, I am getting nowhere.
Island girl, I am scared, don't leave me.

3
Across the bay the streetlamps stare
like amber intersections, and aimlessly
a tree's
shadow splashes the seawall.

The surf turns its pages on dark sand,
the dark boats slip by me as by a lantern,
darkness devours the voices,

And I am an orphaned islander,
on a sandspit of memory,
in a winter
of bays. I have no home.

SOUL ON ICE

Instantly the horizon tilts and sprawls
to a white sky, emptied of geese.
Listen. It seems

years since the ant-trek team
of huskies scrawled across this snow,
leaving no trail, leaving

me, the landscape shimmering, waiting for words.
The syntax of solitude is thickening
my tongue. I cannot bend my back.

What noise is that, the river's roar
or the city's avalanche of words
crashing and breaking far away?

The sun's effort
glows and fades. White napkins
are floating down. Shall I

startle the fossils while yet I think
of trees, white-thighed, whipping about
for our lost love, yours too?

This is our pale vaudeville
so let us dance: the ape's skeleton, erect,
and the ghost. Characters of the

Apocalypse! I am bored
with stares, what I want now
are all those truths the prophets told,

Memory, infancy, where it went wrong,
the ice-flash, the
mastodon, the mastodon!

Listen.
It seems years...

SNOW

Our neighbour's daughter's spun-glass
form does its own thing in
spite of my pane, mirroring
this city's milkwhite lechery.
Our windows tire of facing.
We're double removed, doubly
dead, maybe she knows.
Stays changing her clothes
longer these days, halved by the sill
cleanly. Below that darkening navel I
conjure a mermaid, scaly-tailed.
I suppose we're really at sea.
Glances. For her I am
peevish, am Saturday, that dull
pain she must constantly test her flesh on.
She won't turn her back, her silhouette
knows, the Ripper was black, was black.
I am a clock, climbing to midnight.
"There's a white night between my
house and yours, sister; we were
never meant for each other."
Dreaming is discovering
her, stepped cleanly out of glass,
brazen-breasted, one arm raised,
become, like her London, cold
stone, a crucible, white, implacable
art – then to fold
upright, howling soundlessly, to find
it snowing, the light in her window still on.

TRAFALGAR SQUARE

The sun drifts off, an abandoned balloon
gone high up and cold as a dawn-breaking moon.
The Englishman knows, he'll never look up.
The Labour Government knows. Nelson's no
nearer to heaven these days: framed by his blue
twisting dream of fire, he scythes sadly through
my lifting contempt, your patronage, knowing
Big Ben is higher, and circling still.

Between these I hurry, taut, yet to less
purpose than those pigeons like bull-necked doves,
spinster-fat, waddling for something to love.
If I were a child I would wish to be
a tourist. The pigeons would flock to me.
As is, I wander back
to the fountain, fenced off and beginning to crack,
(the Labour Government knows) where one
stone-breasted mermaid first rose and sailed down
the dolphin-bantering sea around
your childhood, under a molten sun.

So cold now. Moss grows
from her navel and breasts.
If I shared her history, Greek like the rest,
I'd share that foetid anchorage too.
Must keep moving...

The sun's far off, an abandoned balloon
too far for poetry. The Englishman knows.
Give me the moon, I'll pattern it with those
staggering, lost Americans whom
the sad Pacific turned back.

RED HILLS

Hyphen-stretched between Mustang and mule
the road trundles its garbage.
Who'd have thought love was so precise?

We arrive sweating
from the long climb up,
loosen our neckties and lapse

into grins. Red hill scar, red
nigger preserve,
our roses bloom whitely here.

The instamatic transfiguring glare
of TV sunsets, Alsatians.

Each evening, each streetlamp long,
fumbling with padlocks we keep love in
and find no use for memory, though

the figure in the garden,
lost in weed,
bloom towards us with red eyes,

and the unmentionable dog
limp moonward like Santa,
a hole in its head,

favouring its side.

OVERTURE

1

It was not a voice chanting
Ashanti, Ashanti, though the sea
would never stop its hunting

among these barren stones. More
literate than their gods then he rose,
Satanic on this huddled shore

to fuel the flames of loss.
From a height, white wheeling gulls reduced
him, shadow and flesh, to less

than man-sized, and the ocean
towered darkly over him. Yet sun-
light patterning wave still shone

coherent as he blinked, stared:
mirage of a tribe that might yet be
fused. Drawn then to what he feared,

inflamed, he entered water…

2

The ocean is untutored
still, and gulls still pray to the wave's cave.
My father now is minstrel to

an ocean of stones, and no flames lick
about our ankles as sadly we
go down to that sea-music.

WIDE SARGASSO SEA

In memory of Winnifred
and Gertrude Vincent-Brown

Fossilized, itched thin by the worm,
behind plate glass one landscape stays
to haunt my steel age:

a ruined knoll, by a tired sea,
mocks and supports its watermill mashed
like a webbed spider against the sky.

All breeds rust, the worm's lust
mottles that memory, drifts down on us
like clouds on the sun, like

Negroes, in depressed foreground caught
musing over their hoes. Apostrophe-tilted,
they're poised to come

between me and that woman, full-
skirted, on a delicate stroll,
who might have been your grandmother.

The woman's been proven dead
or mad, since. From where I stand, seems no more than
a period on a cobbled stream
where my eyes fasten like tragedy.

A comic opera, conducted by the worm.
I do not claim the bodies, none.
Yet at times, on a ship or fleeing train,

the watermill whirrs within me again,
the sea gleams, the Negroes erupt,
the woman waits by the improbable stile,

and I am the lover between hill and sky,
with one other, going away, caught
at the picture-frame of escape.

Then I break and confess
in a mixed tongue,
an alphabet worn rosary-thin

with the primitive terror that I have been
framed with the rest,
and that each

sunset, when the cardboard galleons come,
my mongoloid brother drums
from time to time on the attic door,

wanting out

wanting in

THE WITNESS

Always when the warring tides
ebb at sunset, someone comes.
At first you can hardly see
him: a black nut in the surf

of the advancing skyline,
or as if the dusk congealed
to fleck that darkening iris:
your eyes widen in terror,

you hate him, mock him as he moves
among the shrapnel of chipped stones,
the palm trees' tattered flags, the stiff
trunks flung face down in the sand…

Later, on the well-lit train
to a colonial future
narrow as rails, you ask "Who
was that stranger by the sea?"

Man, he is your memory,
that each sunset moves among
the jetsam of the tribe, the years,
widowed past grief, yet lingering,

Even as the murmuring
sea unwraps and wraps its arms
in turn around each dead, loved thing:
and the gesture may be fruitless, but is made.

II

PAN SESSION: LAVENTILLE

1

The oildrums submerge. The ebbing
light bears the flotsam of faces away. Dusk
like a threshing of great wings dies
over the city...

2

The god of the surf
is silence

The womb of the wind
is silence

Indeterminate as smoke, thunder rolls from the hills...

Carry in your heart or whisper only:
The sun has been lost at sea.
Carry in your heart: Even now
the gravedigger's banner
hangs from the eaves.

Carry in your heart the canefield's thunder!
Carry in your heart
those quiet seas....

The standpipe's forgotten its function.
Worms play in the bucket beneath it.

Mind yuh face indoors
pickney, pickney,
mind yuh face indoors,
the moon gwine get yuh!

O hear! The city's deserted!
O hear! The corbeau cries
"In the kingdom of carrion Corbeau is King!"
Whose idling furrows the moon's face,
who hangs free now, who is our vanguard –.

Under tides now rising
sand shifts.

The wind's whiplash falls over the city,
the bird's wingspan buries the city,
the moon swerves into eclipse

and night, our village matriarch, ruffling, comes
like any empress between banks of the Nile
clogging the veins of the canals,

while on the hilltop their marble Madonna,
pale as a tombstone in this night's long forgetting,
scythes over the city, toppling,

still sorrowing
in robes.

WHALES

Turning His huge wrist, what spent God,
bent on attrition, let loose these
under the tides' assertions?

Headless
limbless
trunks without names

they surface in our century
from under the ice-maiden's floated smile

or hunger down the valleys of a Gulf whose bile
brings only flotsam back
to our moated city.

The shark in green commercial seas
goes over the decanted poles
and gunwales of our history
where civil salmon ride at ease
and the drowned crew stare from their portholes

but these go down into ancestral darkness.

Where neither gills nor current stalk
these stalk, their flap-mouths and pig-eyes

narrowed for one instruction.

But the God's undone.
Other, steel Leviathans
contradict the sea's tongue,
those sybaritic cadences for home:
and the sky too has been colonised.

Yet, on dark evenings, mesmerised,

something else rises, to mackerel light,
something else makes of its exiled cry
fountains and rainbows!

              The liner churns,
the aircraft, armoured, groans from its lair
for London, Paris, Frankfurt, Rome,
cities of light… their medieval nightmare…

while on the water some great beast
subsides: meanders to comatose
in the God's eye, mute with exhaustion:

winnows

turns
its forehead to the dying sun to die.

THE VISIT

The keskidee calls stubbornly
from the lianas.
A scramble of brambles

tries the shut door.
Nobody in.
Perhaps there's been a gold rush

or something. This is a dead town.
But there's this clock
still ticking. And there's this stable
with the fresh smell of dung. Perhaps they'll be back

soon.
So the stranger on horseback, in formal black,
waited, with an emissary's

patience, while
the clock tocked and the stable dried,
the worms gained, and even the door

fell in suddenly, on a clean, well-lighted
place –
then, as great birds came gliding in

through the stretched jaws
of the valley,
he was sure, and he turned, slapped leather twice,
and rode off, his slowly cantering horse

raising no echoes nor planting the least

hoofprints in the indifferent clay.

THE DARK JURORS

My dark jurors want to know
where I am from: but I am dumb,
finding no syntax to cement
these stones and distant stars,
nor noun but might mash up their monument
of suffering as history.
My jurors are patient. They offer me
a wide range of tongues, like duelling
pistols served on a rattling tray.

VOYAGES

When I am weak and have no cure
to summon up the minotaur,
then, my beloved.

When I am dry as summer's dust
and will not feed a decade's lust,
then, my beloved.

I have travelled far and witnessed many marvellous things:
with Jeffers the ascension of the hawk,
the dead rush of its going; with Lowell
the lily, the rose, the sun on dusk and brick,
the loved, the lover, and their fear of life –
and Derek's mountain wedging its drowned singer –
Spectres and metamorphoses!

To these
I have given up my eyes, my ears, my lungs,
and my hands, they have pocketed them.

And still the generations trod me down!
So history shall carry these away,
no matter how the hawk's head hang in the sunset,
the dawn reiterate all our offerings,
the same sea beat on the seawall.

The poem dies,
the cry in the wake of the slaveship under waves
dies and resurfaces
in a hundred house-and-land simplicities:

in the gaze of that old man, quiet as a stone,
the smile of a child from a shack near Boscobel,
in one bronze girl's awakening –

As if a flower should open in a waste
of memory, or at midnight the mind's prey, startling,
break from its thicket!
When I am weak and have no cure
to summon back the minotaur,
then, my beloved, I

shall vacate this human place
to dock with you, O Apparition,
for our long diminishing

flight to the night

spaces

FACING THE SEA

My unextraordinary small-town girl
in flipflops and a flimsy shift
and a sweater worn like a shawl,

you felt the cold come off the sea,
you squeezed your hands between your thighs,
you stared at the water. You said: "Not me.
I done with this place. I going Kingston."

And in Kingston once, on a sweat-wet bed,
one student nurse, whose name I've forgotten,
sat hugging a pillow and finally said:
"I bored with this place. I going abroad."

Pelicans

creaking on salt-crusted wings,
square-shouldered jets lumbering out,
that cigarette box on the rusty tide,
this frail flotsam of words: all things

travel endlessly outward.

I look at the water and cannot think
Home is where we start from – or
Reaching no absolute in which to rest,
one is always nearer by not keeping still,

until the woman starts up and points.

The floating city that in ropes lay
blazing like iceberg the whole day
is moving now, and though absently

like a hand lifted from memory
to sun-dried eyes, must, in its run,
blot warehouse, factory, market, hillside, sun...

RAMPANALGAS

Rust stiffens the louvres, but we hook
them open a crack for one more look
at the ocean. Overhead, palm trees like hefted squid
lean seaward, trailing their tentacles,
useless in air.

                    We are born here
once only, then like the octopus left
to darken white seas, ink rising through foam,
to print near this beach hut the one word, Home.

Now, years later, I watch this shack,
the heart's first effort, rusting shut,
and turn from the glass. At my back
the ocean tries
the first steps up to this house, and falls back.

THE LAST GAUCHO

For V.S. Naipaul

Time's passed no sentence on his head
crueller than this one: that for him,
being the last, it would never end.
So to pretend, to wake again
those moon-confusing stories told
of cattle and hard-riding men
by the old man with eloquent hands,
how cities sprang up at the train's
coming, or Zapata sank by the wall,
seems to him profitless. Such tales recall
more than an epoch or land, their loss.
So muses the gaucho. How should he know
his time and theirs are an old fiction,
that in the dusk-haze they return
since, centuries ago, in Spain,
Cervantes dreamed the dreamer?
With the night in his hair and his steed's mane
sadly the gaucho crosses the plain.

ROUND TRIP BACK

For the exiled novelists

1
Closing from the sea

past anchored tankers rusting in the rain,
one ketch collapsing canvas, in your lee
the travelling headland and the dull

heave of the bellbuoy goaded by your wash,
its crusted, turtle-
back awash,

the town from memory appears
in the swept, baptismal air:
not as it was —

a grimy port for mariners,
draft-dodgers, intransit visitors,
commissioned writers darkening at the gills,

and home to, say, ten thousand-odd black souls —

but self-contained, monadical and dumb,
some boyhood idyll rusting for the prose

of an elation holier than these,
Melville's,
or Stevenson's, maybe.

O island Eden, by what sea
our romantic agony...

But nearer now, the skiffs that list
cadaverous among the shoals
of garbage drifting ripple-creased

and frayed, like excavated scrolls
from some ephemeral continent –
that severed rock, a monument
the sea reclaimed, an orphanage

now for the transitory gull,
herons, the occasional
pelican: had you forgotten these?

And now your craft's deep tidings shake the pier
and ocean-leaning shanties.
Her house, there…

2

Funny how the past takes place in rain.

Once, a shadow on the beach, you watched
her knotting seines here, vacant, lost.
Composed as a child, yet earthen-eyed,

she was the coast
for which your tossed craft tried.

Now, as in the lacing rain,
all unforgetting things –
this yard, this shack on stilts the weather's honed

to supplicating fingers, that dead tree –
resurface with the boyhood you once owned,

her wet mouth blooms
and vanishes; the wings of her cheekbones
beat in your face!

Her race
abandoned on the Siren's call:
that foam-thighed, apocryphal

nymph who turned into a weir,
into another country,
your grinding, sickening landfall over there...

3
Once more the ship is moving and the heart's
coherence trembles, trembles and departs
as the bow wave mounts. From the stern

you watch the wake, its compass that must widen
however groundswells run, the heart stiffen,

to an arc describing "village",
a bay's mouth miming "home",
and turn

as a late sun gilds the rooftops of the poor,
and wharf, post office, market, Shorty's Bar,
shine like staked martyrs...

Leave that alone.
The ocean rolling sideways on its chain,
disgorges its bereavement, but our first stars

have swum clear, growing lucid in their pain.
The headland ends,

the landgrown, landbound
love goes into declension where
the lives you left meander to the sea.

So, sleep.
This coast shall keep you, grounded though you tread
in nightmare now across some whitening plain

or insubstantial city, whom the snow
shall numb beyond our waning love or pity,

who cannot cry, forgive us, for the rain.

A LETTER FROM ELIZABETH

You! after all these years
                    (Here, fingers
of the waking mind, frisking its album, come upon
her planted stance, hands anchored on her hips,
that glazed, insouciant, myopic grin –

Nudger and tugger, sailfish on the move,
where others spoke at grave length she rained words
then stopped bemusedly, her startled thought
flown off to crouch beneath some mossy stone).

She writes:
"You will be pleased (I hope!) for me –
Your 'sis' has gone and got herself engaged
to this guy from Howard (smiles!)"

I smile, remembering, another time
the wings of some absurdity
flew across her watchful face;
her instant pealing echoing laugh
shattered the darkened cinema.

"Would you believe that I don't like to think
back on those times, primarily
because then I feel really sad,
really feel it, deep down?"

How can I answer her, who answered me
so many ways,
whom now the same precocious spring betrays?
Say that time passes only to return?
Or utter that belated fiction that
time saddens, true, but also makes us wise?

I could have lived forever in her gaze
as in a sunstruck, languorous season.

My sorrow, all I have for you are words
and they are fickle sailors; but I know
that what is spoken cannot be unspoken
however the bright thought tarnish in the sand.

The tree we raised has fallen and made trees,
and somewhere off your coast, near Blanchisseuse,
a rocking acre holds this image still:

you wading in, all gooseflesh, squeals and wails,
me, tight-lipped, following; then both of us
pausing, as if sensing, even then,
the far advance and rumble of these lines
I write in desolation for you now.

IN REAL LIFE

There are ledges where the water
italicises the dead trunk,

there is a verandah the salt wind
has whitened with fictions,

and from these, in real life,
she would get up dusting
her bottom and grinning *hello* or
in another mood

come and lay a cool palm flat
on the dry mat
of his chest.

Now, bodiless,

she drifts through him as though
by night a warm rain-bearing wind
were stealing among saplings.

He has read through the night, one whose fictions
are consolations of the night,
yet feels in his pores some slow

cloud palming each star,
whole
constellations of stars,

(and how silent, ah, how secret
that decimation of starlight!)

Still to call the ocean
"ocean" without her, strive
to save with these few props —

a shack, a salt cliff, and a sea
so blue it should blind that syllable —

her from the embalming light!

He writes of her abashed
smile of admission, her look
of entry and alarm,
and of salutation,

writing, "there are ledges,"
fading into the
writing, until morning
darkens with alarm

clocks and his next-door neighbour's wife,
drifting across glass,
sees nothing there: a desk, a chair,

while elsewhere, in real life
through strengthening light strolling —

droll commas tugging at her mouth,
the averted cat's-eyes slit with glee —
her tinkling laugh absolves them both

to a surf stately and thunderous.

POEM WITHOUT END

...if I talked to a fern do you think it would
answer   if I stopped at your window what...
(Tony McNeill: "The Catherine Poem")

If I could write a poem
not like a wall of icons
a poem that would flitter   dip   veer
swallow among chandeliers

would your child's heart slip from its carapace
would your cat's-eyes follow

If I could bring you near
as a jeweller brings some veined
translucent stone   and hold you there

would you walk in the old ways   quick among ferns
would your pale breasts thaw from the marble

Catherine   name from the north
name of the waif among mansions
of the almond-eyed girl in the rose garden

I write with the night in my veins
the secretive midnight sea
stirs the same stones   by the same sea-almonds
where once you blessed with your hands

who thought I would write such a poem

that someone   somewhere in the world
but you are silent   and this night
of your absence is cold   cold

PARADIGM

1 (*The siege*)

If I were twice the man, or half,
you'd not suffer so.
A lesser would have torn you down,
a greater let you go.

But in me God and beast have been
so maddeningly mixed
(as love would have us, each in each
irrevocably lost!)

that I who would not for the world
bring sorrow upon your head,
a widening of that grave gaze,
confusion to your bed,

must like a double negative
unsheathing, stand apart,
and watch myself lay secret siege
to your embattled heart.

2

You say it is forbidden —
tell me to stop, then.
But do not try to arbitrate
where love should end.

Old men have in their dotage dreamed,
schoolboys have loved the sea,
though dreaming never cured old age,
and the sea is no one's friend.

3

Others have called this continence
sweet sorrow – I cannot –
though God knows – if you're happy –
there's that.

4

You swore indulgent Adam
betrayed his wanton Eve,
that their platonic paradise
might yet have been preserved
had Adam been more adamant.
(*You said so. You said so.*)

Then tell me, adamantine girl,
now that our time has gone,
and we have been, O blameless
as islands in the sun,
why must we take for Eden
the dark side of the moon?
(*You said so. You said so.*)

5 (*On being pestered for a letter*)

You warned that, being spoken for
to all the listening world,
I should not speak, must be content
if dreams alone paroled
me from your indifference –
and, woman, that was fair.

Yet now you doubt my silence
and interrogate my sleep!

RAMON REMEMBERS

Three pilgrims passed here one October night,
one of those nights of windfall and the moon
arriving late through separating cloud.
They came into the moonlight from the wood.

I remember the heavy shining of their robes
and their strange mules, the hump-backed, long-necked ones.
Men walking watch the earth, but these looked up
and on their parchment faces doubt and awe
played for possession.
                              The moon kept up
its patient expurgation of the grass,
its bulge-eye roundly stared; but what they saw
if not the moon, some torn cloud and some stars
in my unsubtle heaven, heaven knows.
Dispassionate as ants they crossed the field.

And, yes, I should have called out; there are laws
of trespass, after all, a man had cause
enough to wring a reason from their calm:
destinations, occupations, home towns, names.
I did not call,
I stood and watched in silence, like a fool.

So where in the end they got to, what they sought,
I cannot tell, and would not think it worth
the while to go enquiring about.
Their business was the nightsky, mine, the earth.

Yet there've been darkening afternoons, since then,
that I've looked up from where the horse's hoof
arrows the bumping plough and seen them there,
stray-footed, hesitant, wearing that same air

of dubious obedience to a sign
eye could not fathom nor commonsense descry,

And ignorance of their ending sets me free
to think them unarriving, drifting still
(a thought which, for some reason, gladdens me)
over the storied mountains, through the world.

RAMON'S DREAM

1

I woke to a forest in fog: grey,
grey-blue the trees, and

birdless. So, if what they say
of matter and all that is true,

something new
must have been born

elsewhere to balance this blue
absence of birdsong, and flight.

Whatever it is must be huge!
(This silence feels like forever)

2

Maybe was born in the night.
Maybe that roar like a river

of blood in the ear was the white
gelatinous sea rolling over

to deliver itself of a future
one-eyed and tall as – who knows?

One thing I can tell:
from these rows
of washed-out trees, this shell
of a moon something's sucked and discarded,

whatever it is, it eats light.

THE LOVERS

And they are gone: aye, ages tong ago
These lovers fled away into the storm.
(Keats: "The Eve of St. Agnes")

She says *My life is yours* and means *I fear,*
He says *I shall protect you* and means *own*;
now they are cantering westward. Her set stare,
rock-still, belies the animal she rides,
his face is all in shadow. On both sides
one darkness waits for them. I watch them run
until they are lights on water, fading, gone.
Now they are gone, what silences close after?
Will they ride on, in the storm's eye forever,
its dream? Or wake in time and, waking, wither?
How will they learn to breathe again
air without rain?

WORDS

for his estranged wife

Everything revolved at first, then settled
to an elate stillness.
You move, pristine through memory,
a stranger I have always known,
big-boned and careless and capable,
likelier than I was to stand than run,
pursued now by two dreamless daughters.
The only people in the world
you could never outface or outwait!
I know this is inappropriate,
that these lines, splaying, miss the ground
where you dream, a distracted, vague tree
or felon for her freedom,
and think that there must be ways to give
back what you gave.
But the sentence stands. We never found
words in which we could both live.

SONG FOR A LADY

> *Weep not, child,*
> *Weep not, my darling,*
> *With these kisses let me remove your tears,*
> *The ravening clouds shall not long be victorious,*
> *They shall not long possess the sky...*
>   (Whitman: "On the Beach at Night")

You wanted at first just the simple romances,
evenings of amber and bird-happy dawns,
they gave you a whip and a tunic of thorns

Weep not, child

You wanted then drums and improbable dances
and the loud sun to punish your body black
they gave you a map and an almanac

Weep not, child

You cried, "But the yellow moon advances
and I am no longer young!"
They cried when they saw what the moon had done,
they cried, "She was lovely once and strong,"
They cried, "She was lovely once but wrong for us!"

Weep not, child

For there is a grave, ineluctable music
rises at times from their gardens of stances.
You are that gravity. You are that music.

Weep not, child

SONG FOR A TOURIST

When upon this fabled beach
you in nightmare rise to watch
twilit lives enact their fate

and the stars eliminate
oiled civility and touch
(make no lyric memories)

passion's faggot where it lies,
while the blood-dark ocean cries
"Walk softly, danger, danger!"

Make no lyric memories.
Stranger, these are Siren Isles.
Make no lyric memories

stranger, stranger, stranger!

WINTERSONG

for Jeni

The fire's baffled, fitful snarl
inside, outside the snow –
it seemed she'd landed in some quarrel
whose terms she didn't know.

She'd seen the sea rise up and whack
upon a wall, the wall
rise up and hurl the ocean back –
she swore she'd seen it all

and thanked God that she had survived
that war of sea and stone,
not dreaming how the years arrived
now how she'd come to learn

that such impassioned combatants
grow pale before the snow's
indifferent, noiseless argument,
the fire's stubborn rose.

THE BLACK TREE

He stood with the woman in his arms
where the lane, veering, plunged its black
snakeskin gleam smoothly between sentries of amber
till it lost volition to an amber haze
and felt his blood thicken.
                          He listened
as a tree listens
for the lightest stirrings of its nerves
at the midges' news, through the cavernous roar
of sap in its slow veins,

and as the woman in his arms
buried her face against the glare
of headlamps lunging sideways from their high cave,

he heard, distinctly as a tree hears
rain in the black hills feelering near,
the tumult of approaching war,

and he saw Earth as she would be
when it was done: weak, grinning and
dazedly rising, but still one
with the ponderous, serene and stoneblind spheres.

These things he felt, heard and saw
in his thirty-sixth year,
standing, without fear or hope,
with a girl from his island quiet in his arms

beneath pale cloud, in Europe.

ENGLAND, AUTUMN

*Perhaps one should say truthfulness rather than truth in order to purge it of
the high-flying or high-flown sonority which Larkin is so sceptical of.*

(Christopher Ricks)

But, doesn't heaven
prophesy still over England?
Since when was lightning ironic,
or thunder without sonority?

You ought to walk with me, critic,
you should not have to ask
your old houseboy, returning, to translate the wind,

don't you know that, however composed
into eloquent postures,
these drystone walls, these hedgerows
are less than the rage that made them?

You should ask more of literature,
not sceptical, ask it the wind's name,
ask Prospero that, ask Satan, aye,

and ask any glad-eyed, terrified
hare whom the moor discloses
if Truth, high-flying, doesn't still

on occasion stoop from a smoking sky,
or an imperilled, mortal "I"
break from your carapaced "one".

You could still say "Man" and make the walls fall down;
ask that felon lit by horizon!

Or walk with me, mister, walk with me, sir,
through any starched maternity
wing, with its silence of libraries,

with its doctors like dry undertakers,
and watch
as some tiny, rage-suffused

warrior, your "first Englishman",
medalled in mucus and ribboned in blood,
crashes into the light now, and like this

bad, unkempt, distempered poem

glares around him, bellowing

CRITIC

Takes rain, the racket
in a madman's head
                    and strains
it into sonata.

Takes sea, the dumb cry
in a madman's throat
                    and whips up
white horses of words.

Through virgin forests
he pounds a clear path
                    the ignoble savage
might follow. Always, who followed

came to this camp:
raw treetrunks, black
                    smoking coals.
Some camped, those wiser turned back.

Till one who went further,
past the path's end,
                    made one last bend
uphill and came

out of the rained-out dark upon
this stalled station wagon,
                    its headlamps still
silently shafting the silent pines.

QUINAM BAY

In memory of Eric Roach
and after reading the eulogies

1
Roach gone, the carrion
that drove him, hurt hawk, from the echoing air
with their hunger for bloodbath, their shrill caws
of treachery,
shriek with excitement.
Dead, and to them he is Hero.
Carrion like them dead.

But if, or for how long, he tread
that narrowing haven, observing
the sheer light of those first words fail
in their fustian heaven,

nobody knows
or will, now.
Love overgrows a rock,
but not a raftload of schisms.

2
At Quinam Bay, when the tide goes,
the ocean upholds itself
stilly, without contradiction,
and it is the sky that shatters.

Diarist, there are matters
best left to these birds and the sand's blowing.
Walk softly here.

And do not talk of the hawk on the air,
or of the plankton's release from its drifting.
Spare him the folk he could not save.
Leave out the landscape he loved.

However green the shoreline,
however blue the sky,
face down he came to the beach.

But rest him in language unadorned
as bread, there where the ocean fed
him back to the shore he turned from,

not free, free at last, carrion,
but locked
in his tiring dream of destruction,

with his head full of salt,
his lost craft,
nothing, his destination.

TRANSPARENT THINGS

There was the day when I began to doubt
Man's sanity: How could he live without
Knowing for sure what dawn, what death, what doom
Awaited consciousness beyond the tomb?
(Vladimir Nabokov: *Pale Fire.*)

Suddenly to write, in this dread hour,
Nabokov dead, that the word lives –
What is that? Ambition?

They are beyond ambition
who walk toward that mountain,

Then why am I urged
to punctuate this pause
in the iambic breathing of the world,
heart-stopped, with the blood of fable?

Silence would be truer,
you left the world completed, after all,

Yet while they circle aimlessly, the words,
above the body of the fallen master,
butterflies blown from some oblivious grove,

I am moved from nature's metaphors to praise.

O Clown Prince of Russia, they survive, they survive,
your stationary sunset,
the lindens, the rose,

and the pale moon.

THE BIND

All young men dream,
but, at thirty-five,
isn't it time you learned?

What you can lose will be lost.

What they cannot take
from you is the pain
of loss, the enduring pearl of pain –

that is yours,
till you learn to live at last
without such punctual heartbreak.

Then they will take that too.

PROSE

Now that he is dead she wanders on
through rooms that, in anticipation
of a full house he'd bought her, oh,
forty years ago.
Their marriage was a hard one,
they had no children,
and he became a nuisance as he aged.
She'd have to sit and listen while he raged
on about the young, the unions, friends.
She'd nod, or shake her head and look away.
'Ah, Tommy!' she'd say.

A saddening home, you claim: *unrhyming lives
complaining not for poetry but plain prose*,
and I'd be apt to listen; but one scene
keeps curling, like the wavecurl a rock throws
in fast declining water, in my mind.

He'd been away,
and we at the docks were waiting. When he came
she moved to meet him, hurrying,
and they clung together, briefly making one
in the shadow of the great ship looming there
already fuelling to turn and go.

A scene out of some album, long ago
when love like life seemed boundless (till time halved
it), of promise not yet unfulfilled?

No,
for his feet faltered all the way
down the long gangplank; and her hair,
when wind or his unsteady hand unscarved it,
was already grey.

AUTUMN ELEGY

Neruda, Casals

1

Dead in one month, the two Pauls,
while overhead as usual
squirrels work the acorn tree
and the sun
wanders.

Dead, and together they
draw nearer. One
huddles a domed skull against the weather,
but slow-eyed, reverential,
as if he crouched to listen, not to play;
the other from his windy highway moves…

Mere
shades, mere sketches
for the sun's distraction, what had they
in common but this wilderness of air,
a glare like autumn's pressuring the leaves
– their earthward-dreaming flush! – to pierce each chord
or speechless scene, the heart hushed for its name,
as when, death-pierced, Quixote whispered "Spain!"
and that to monumental form
they raised the natural man?

The autumn haze prospecting in the wall
raises its brief gold. Their faces turn,
incredulous as Mary's or struck Saul,
into the blade of sunlight glancing down.

2

And what if time should lose their names
to fires that the guns decree,
or pedagogue uproot some theme
from that organic harmony
whose music circles all, now light, now grave,
whose name is love?

They have become the heart of what they praised,
and as the flaking sun redeems its gold,
as the tree forgets its litter and the dawn,
its mother, murmurs, "Child, it is the world,"
they tremble towards utterance.

Within this pause that flowers, like the wave
towering for its syllable, that calm curve
some lens forever renders, let them live,
autumnal as this acorn tree whose leaves
turn to the encroaching dark their sun

until imagination make them one.

THE BRIEFING

Say goodbye to Earth,
you will not see her again.
Carry her therefore in your heart
as in your blood: without estrangement.
You will not reach the stars,
nor your son, nor your son's son,
and yet that realm of perpetual light
is your destination.
May your flight be faultless and your hand
obey you at the last.
May you find your lost companions.
May your death be without pain.
Now say goodbye to Earth.
Thirty minutes ten seconds and counting...

ABOUT THE AUTHOR

Born in Trinidad in 1944, Wayne Brown read English at the University of the West Indies in Jamaica and lived mainly between the two countries until his death in 2009. His books include *On The Coast* (Andre Deutsch, 1972) which was awarded the Commonwealth Prize for Poetry, and was a Poetry Book Society recommendation; *Edna Manley: The Private Years* (Andre Deutsch, 1976), a biography of the Jamaican sculptress; a second volume of poems, *Voyages* (Inprint Caribbean, 1989); and *The Child of the Sea* (Inprint Caribbean, 1990), like his later *Landscape with Heron* (Observer Literary Books, 2000), a collection of short stories and remembrances. He edited *Derek Walcott: Selected Poetry* (Heinemann Caribbean, 1981) and edited and produced several anthologies of Jamaican fiction and poetry.

Wayne Brown was a Gregory Fellow in Poetry at the University of Leeds, England, a Fulbright Scholar in the US, and a Fellow of Yaddo, MacDowell, The Virginia Center for the Creative Arts, and the Rockefeller Foundation. He lectured in English Literature in the US and at both the Trinidadian and Jamaican campuses of the University of the West Indies. Between 1984 and 2009, some 3,500 editions of his column "In Our Time" appeared in Trinidadian and Jamaican newspapers; and between February and November 2008 he wrote a weekly column, "The Race for the White House", which appeared in the Sunday editions of the *Trinidad Express*, the *Nation* (Barbados) and the *Stabroek News* (Guyana). For six months in 2009 he wrote a column called "In the Obama Era", before returning to his original, wide-ranging column, "In Our Time".

Wayne Brown was editor of the literary pages of the *Sunday Observer* and the *Sunday Gleaner* and was the founder-tutor of The Creative Writing Workshop. He also tutored in Creative Writing (fiction, non-fiction and poetry) in the Low-residency MFA Creative Writing program of Lesley University, MA; taught Creative Writing (Poetry) at the UWI, Mona; and taught an online creative writing course for Stanford University. His two daughters, Mariel and Saffrey, live in Trinidad and Jamaica respectively.

ALSO BY WAYNE BROWN

The Scent of the Past and Other Stories
ISBN:9781845231538; pp. 442; December 2010; £14.99

If one wanted to find out what Trinidad and the Caribbean has been like in the last decades of the 20th century, there would be no better place to look than the stories in this collection. Whilst many of the writers of his generation reconstructed the Caribbean world from distance and memory, publishing primarily for a metropolitan audience, Brown's stories began as publications in his weekly newspaper column with a very substantial popular audience. But there is nothing ephemeral about this work, because Brown invests these pieces with all a major poet's delight in the power of language and with a craftsman's meticulous for their structure as short stories. Frequently, the line between fiction and actuality is deliberately blurred as Brown invokes the shaping light of memory to resurrect the people and places he has known or loved (or merely imagined). Wayne Brown is no less a character in these fictions than Philip Roth and his various avatars is in his. What one has in the collection is a striking ability to portray people and tell stories that are particular and unique, but which cohere to form an unrivalled portrait of a rapidly changing society.

OTHER CARIBBEAN MODERN CLASSICS

Now in print: